AFTER COVID-19 WHAT? -

MOVE FORWARD:
SERVE WITH EXCELLENCE!

AFTER COVID-19 WHAT? -

MOVE FORWARD:
SERVE WITH EXCELLENCE!

DR. SAMUEL U. DANIEL PHD

XULON PRESS

Xulon Press
2301 Lucien Way #415
Maitland, FL 32751
407.339.4217
www.xulonpress.com

© 2022 by Dr. Samuel U. Daniel PhD

All rights reserved solely by the author. The author guarantees all contents are original and do not infringe upon the legal rights of any other person or work. No part of this book may be reproduced in any form without the permission of the author. The views expressed in this book are not necessarily those of the publisher.

Due to the changing nature of the Internet, if there are any web addresses, links, or URLs included in this manuscript, these may have been altered and may no longer be accessible. The views and opinions shared in this book belong solely to the author and do not necessarily reflect those of the publisher. The publisher therefore disclaims responsibility for the views or opinions expressed within the work.

Unless otherwise indicated, Scripture quotations taken from the King James Version (KJV) – *public domain.*

Scripture quotations taken from the Amplified Bible (AMP). Copyright © 1954, 1958, 1962, 1964, 1965, 1987 by The Lockman Foundation. Used by permission. All rights reserved.

Paperback ISBN-13: 978-1-6628-4728-8
Ebook ISBN-13: 978-1-6628-4729-5

Acknowledgments

I am grateful to God for His mercies, love, and grace extended to me over the years. He is indeed faithful! My fellow ministerial colleagues, the leadership team, and the congregants of the Church of God of Prophecy Anguilla, must be commended for the inspiration and the stimuli they provided in getting this work written. Nearer home, I wish to thank my family members for their love and support throughout this project. My spouse, Malita, and my children, Jervayne and Samalta, have all been understanding and provided constant encouragement to complete the manuscript. Indeed, they are a collective gift from God.

Dedication

This book was written as an encouragement to every person who has experienced loss during the COVID-19 pandemic and somehow feel retarded in their efforts to move forward. Be encouraged to move beyond your pain and disappointment, and embrace a brighter future with God, as you serve with excellence.

Contents

Acknowledgments vii
Dedication ix
Preface xiii

1. Move Forward: Prepare Your Mind to Remember 1
2. Move Forward: Allow the Word to Shape You 11
3. Move Forward: Crossover 29
4. Move Forward with Hope 39
5. Move Forward: Look to Jesus for Healing 53
6. Move Forward: Serve with Excellence 67
7. Move Forward: Get Under the Cloud of God 83
8. Move Forward by Putting God First . . 103
9. Move Forward: Acknowledge God as Your Refuge and Strength 113

About the Author 127

Preface

The greater part of this volume presents a keen focus on the book of Deuteronomy. Deuteronomy means "the second law" or "the repetition of the law." You see, the law was first given to the Israelites at Mt. Sinai. But the first generation of believers proved to be a sinful people, a people of unbelief and disobedience. They did not believe God, not enough to lay hold of the Promised Land. As a result, they wandered about for forty years and died in the desert wilderness. Now forty years later, Moses, this aged servant of God, stands before the second generation of believers—the sons and daughters of the unbelieving generation—and repeats the law to them. For a second time, he seeks to prepare a generation of believers to enter the Promised Land. This is what Deuteronomy is about.

So then, the great book of Deuteronomy is a series of messages preached by Moses as he sought to prepare the second generation of Israelites to enter, conquer, and possess the Promised Land. This is my aim as we traverse the contents of this book series. As a people, I want to propel us forward toward our spiritual Promised Land, so that we can serve our God in excellence, in light of the havoc COVID-19 reaped universally over the passing two years! In essence, God's people must regain pose, momentum, and focus as we consider the question: after COVID-19, what? —as we serve our God with excellence.

Note the meaning of some key terms we will use in this book.

- **Moving** speaks of motion, of change; changing one's position.
- **Forward** speaks of progress; progressive, positive motion. It speaks of changing one's static position and going onwards, so as to make progress. Forward also speaks of being in a position of prominence or notice. It conveys the idea of facing the front; progressing towards a successful conclusion. Forward means advancing positively.

- **Serving** speaks of performing duties or services for someone (in this case, God). It carries the idea of attending to a customer or providing services for a customer.
- **Excellence** is the quality of being extremely good or outstanding. It is a quality that describes God's standards. God is excellent! And God, who is extremely good, wants us to move forward as a people, displaying His attributes.

He wants us to get into motion and progress toward a position of spiritual prominence into that place in Him where we attend to His business with extremely high and exceptional standards. He wants us to forget the failures, forget the fears, forget the mistakes of the past, and move forward in our relationship with Him. In the words of the apostle Paul: "forgetting those things which are behind, and reaching forth unto those things which are before ... press toward the mark for the prize of the high calling of God in Christ Jesus" (Phil. 3:13–14). Despite the various challenges of the passing years, the apprehensions and ravages of COVID-19 and the universality of political upheavals, the brazen encouragement is for the believer to keep going, to move forward with our lives and our service to humankind. The challenge to us is to advance in the ministry that Jehovah has ordained for us in this season. So, let us begin *Moving Forward: Serving with Excellence!*

Chapter One

Move Forward: Prepare Your Minds to Remember

"The Lord our God spake unto us in Horeb, saying, Ye have dwelt long enough in this mount: turn and take your journey, and go" (Deut. 1:6–7a KJV).

Confession: *With God's help, I will move forward in my spiritual life by making earnest preparations to succeed! I must prepare my mind! I must learn from my past; I must remember!*

Introduction

Let us begin by observing the meaning of the term *preparation*. This is the action or process of making ready or being made ready. It is that important step that quickens our minds to achieve. Preparation is that necessary step that gives one the capacity to embrace success. Put another way, if you are not prepared, success may come your way and you may not be able to handle it for, as Idowu Koyenikan said: "Opportunity does not waste time with those who are unprepared." Preparation is what would enable a person to welcome and embrace opportunities when they come; and as H. Jackson Brown Jr. puts it: "The best preparation for tomorrow is doing your best today."

Despite the global pessimism amidst the pandemic, by the mercies and authority of a gracious God, we have been ushered into a new year 2022. This is a year that many feel, that despite the challenges, God is waiting to pour His perfect vision into His people, so that we can champion His cause for the ending of time. The previous years, for many of us, were unimaginable. But this year is envisaged as a year in which some will witness God's increased favor, notwithstanding great challenges. This means that we must take time and prepare ourselves early for the blessings as well as for the battles that this year holds. I believe that part of the greatest preparations one can make to face this year is to give serious consideration to the state of his/her mind. For scripture affirms that "as [a man] thinketh in his heart, so is he" (Prov. 23:7a KJV). And the apostle Paul advocating change, encourages: "And be not conformed to this world: but be ye transformed (be changed) *by the renewing of your mind*, that ye may prove what is that good, and acceptable, and perfect, will of God" (Rom. 12:2 KJV).

This tells me that lasting change must first come from the mind. This also tells me that our actions feed from what we conceive and treasure in our minds. Our successes and failures must first germinate in our minds. Our victories and our defeats must first take place in our minds before they come into reality. Therefore, our preparations to move forward in excellence toward our spiritual Promised Land has to be first conceived in our minds.

Tell somebody: If we are going to move forward and serve God in excellence, we have to first change our minds!

To succeed, we must change the negativity that the enemy would bring to our minds and replace it with positive thoughts! We must change our defeatist mentality (that says we can't do it) to that of the overcomer that God says we are (by thinking: I can do all things through Christ who gives me strength)! We must hold fast to Paul's admonition to the Philippians: "Whatsoever things are true, whatsoever things are honest, whatsoever things are just, whatsoever things are pure, whatsoever things are lovely, whatsoever things are of good report; if there be any virtue, and if there be any praise, think on these things" (Phil. 4:8 KJV).

We must retrain our minds to think positively! Tell somebody: We have to think positively this year! And this positive thinking must begin with our memory. We must prepare ourselves by training our minds to remember. How often do we forget? But in 2022, we must remember God! We must remember the character of our God! We must remember the power of our God! We must remember God!

God had delivered the Israelites from the enslavement of Egypt (which is a symbol of the world), and He had led them through forty years of wilderness wanderings. This has been seen in the great books of Exodus and Numbers.

Chapter One

The book of Numbers closed with the Israelites camped in the plains of Moab close by the Jordan River, across from the great city of Jericho. At last, they were poised to enter the Promised Land of God. But before they could cross the Jordan to lay claim of their promised inheritance, they had to be prepared—spiritually prepared. Spiritual preparation is the thrust of the great book of Deuteronomy. To prepare the people, Moses preached a series of messages that were grouped under three basic subjects:

1. The need to remember the lessons from history (1:6–4:43).

History provides powerful encouragement for the believers. For we understand that if God did it in the past, He can do it again. By learning from the past, the Israelites would know how to conquer the Promised Land and build a strong, orderly society within the land. They were called to remember the lessons from their past. To remember was a recurring theme in the book of Deuteronomy. One of the places it can be seen is in Deuteronomy 15:15 (KJV) where we read: "And thou shalt remember that thou wast a bondman in the land of Egypt, and the Lord thy God redeemed thee: therefore I command thee this thing to day."

And doesn't that sound familiar? A great part of our spiritual success this year is tied to our memory. We must remember God! We must remember the many times and in the many ways that God came through for us in 2019, 2020 and 2021 during the novel and aggressive spread of the coronavirus. We must remember how He delivered us! We must remember how He provided protection for us! We must remember how He healed our bodies! We must remember how He kept us from evil by His mighty hands!

We must remember how He fought for us; and brought us through in years gone by! We must remember the goodness of God! We must remember (in John Newton's "Amazing Grace") that "Through many dangers, tolls and snares, we have already come; 'Tis grace hath brought us safe thus far, and grace will lead me home!" (gospelweb.net).

Remembering is necessary for moving forward with faith. Remember your spiritual history! Remember God!

2. The need to remember the Ten Commandments and the laws that are to govern man and society (4:44–26:19).

The Israelites had to know and obey the law to please God. They had to know the law in order to live victorious and fruitful lives, and to build a just and righteous society. If we are to experience success as we journey through the 2020s, we must remember the guiding principles of God's Word. God to Joshua admonished: "This book of the law shall not depart out of thy mouth; but thou shalt meditate therein day and night, that thou mayest observe to do according to all that is written therein: for then thou shalt make thy way prosperous, and then thou shalt have good success" (Josh. 1:8 KJV).

We must remember the Word this year! Don't neglect the Word this year. Prosperity is in the Word! The principles for good success are in the Word!

To move forward towards your spiritual Promised Land in this season, you must give God's Word its rightful place in your life! You must take the time to read, study, and digest it. We must remember those commandments and laws that would help us to live as God has designed for us to live! We must treasure the promises God has provided for us in His Word for our benefit. Despite our busy schedules, we must give God's Word priority! We must spend time in God's Word in this season, if we are to experience the wisdom of God's leadership. Paul, to his spiritual son Timothy, admonished: "Study to shew thyself approved unto God, a workman that needeth not to be ashamed, rightly dividing the word of truth" (2 Tim. 2:15 KJV). Studying God's Word would cause you to gain God's approval. And to be approved by God, places you ahead in life. Why? Because wisdom is in the Word!

3. The charge to rededicate their lives to God, to renew their covenant, or commitment with God (27:1–30:20).

Once the Israelites had been led to recommit their lives to God, then and only then would they be ready to inherit the Promised Land of God. God is ready to usher us into a new dimension in Him. He wants so much to reveal His power and authority to us as His people. He wants to pour out a fuller measure of His anointing in our midst. But He is waiting for us to earnestly rededicate ourselves to Him. He is waiting for us to renew our covenant with Him. After all, we cannot pour new wine into old wine skins, lest they stretch and burst. And God cannot pour fresh anointing into old vessels. He wants us to renew our capacity to receive Him and His fresh revelations in this new season while the world is filled with so much uncertainty. During the times of "lock down" in our various territories, God provided us with opportunities to seek His face, rededicate ourselves, and be renewed in our inner man with spiritual impetus for our journey. Only when we in earnestly rededicate ourselves to God; only when we renew our covenant and commitment to God, would He be able to propel us forward, into our spiritual Promised Land—the spiritual place where He wants us to be!

Conclusion

And so, as I close this chapter and consider how this world is shifting, I ask: What is your desire in this new season? Is it any different from the previous years? Are you satisfied with your spiritual life? Now that you are fully aware of just how our world can change in an instant; now that we have seen so many of our relatives and friends succumb to COVID-19 all over the world, do you have any ambition to move forward and serve God with greater sincerity? How willing are you to rededicate your life to Christ? How much effort are you willing to make to change your mind-set and renew your covenant with God? At this start of this new era, I pray that your spiritual desire be fulfilled.

Chapter Two

Move Forward: Allow the Word to Shape You

"The Lord our God spake unto us in Horeb, saying, Ye have dwelt long enough in this mount:" (Deut. 1:6 KJV).

Confession: *If I am to move forward in my spiritual life in this new era, I must allow the Word of God to shape me!*

Introduction

When we ended the last chapter, Israel was liberated, freed from the slavery of Egypt, and they were chosen by God to be His very special people. They were to be a nation of people who would be His witnesses to the immoral and unrighteous of the earth. Marching out of Egypt, the Israelites were a nation of people whose king was God, Himself. But they had no constitution that legally formed them into a nation and no land to call their home. The constitution was drawn up at Mt. Sinai, a constitution (covenant) that was to govern the relationship between the people and their King. The form of government established by the constitution or covenant was a theocracy. This means that God, Himself was the one in charge, the King, the wonderful Ruler who had saved the Israelites from the terrible fate of slavery and death in Egypt (which is a symbol of the world). Therefore, the people owed their lives to God. They were to be the subjects of the Ruler who had so graciously saved them, the subjects of God, Himself.

Let me pause here to remind us that regardless of what is happening in your life and in the world, Jehovah God is still King! He is the one in charge, the wonderful Ruler who saved us from the terrible fate of the slavery of sin and from the end result of death in the world. Therefore, as a people, we owe our lives to God. The scripture tells us: "For we are His people and the sheep of His pasture" (Ps. 95:7). That is why we are to "enter into His gates with thanksgiving and into His courts with praise" (Ps. 100:4). God's goodness is seen in His deliverance from sin and the provision of His full and free salvation. Somebody needs to praise Him for that!

And so, this was the history of Israel's birth, the formation of Israel as a theocratic nation, that is, a nation ruled by God, Himself. The Israelites had their King and their constitution. Now, they were soon to receive the inheritance of their land, the great promise of God. They now stood ready to enter the Promised Land. But as we emphasized in chapter one, they had to be prepared to do so. They had to allow the Word of God to shape them.

If we are to make significant strides in our spiritual lives this year, if we are to move forward spiritually as a people in any way at all, we must give way to the Word and allow it to take root in our hearts and lives. Our own ideas and philosophies won't do! Our personal feelings or opinions won't help us. Our traditional practices and customs just won't cut it. Any spiritual gains we make this year has to be because we adhere to the principles of the Word of God and allow them to do a work in our lives. Put another way, we would have to live what the Word says this year! This is our emphasis in this chapter: moving forward and making earnest preparations to succeed—*Allowing the Word to Shape You*!

So, how do we allow the Word to shape us? From looking at our passage, there seems to be two main considerations:

A. Being Receptive of God's Messengers

The Children of Israel were about ready to lay hold on the Promised Land, but they needed some final instructions. This means that they had to have someone to give them these instructions. And this was the messenger, Moses, the servant of God. As the messenger of God, Moses was a symbol of both Christ and the minister of God. Moses was chosen by God:

- to be the liberator of Israel, freeing them from Egyptian slavery;
- to be the great leader of Israel, leading them toward the Promised Land; and

- to be the founding father of Israel as a nation; and to be the intercessor who stood between God and His people.

But this was not all. God also chose Moses to be the messenger of God, the great giver and communicator of the law of God. It is this call, this function of Moses—to be the messenger of God—that is one of the major foci of the great book of Deuteronomy. As mentioned in the first chapter, God had three sermons—three strong challenges—that He wanted declared to His people. In obedience to God, the messenger of God was to stand boldly before the people and preach the sermons. This is one of the great scenes of the book of Deuteronomy: Moses standing and preaching three sermons, three strong challenges to the people of God. And if the people were to benefit from the message from God, the people would have to *be receptive of God's message through His messenger.* Let me tell you that it is impossible to receive the message without receiving the messenger. For the message and the messenger are one.

Herein lies the struggle of many in the church in their quest to move forward spiritually, and herein lies the reason why many are often sick and struggle to prosper – disrespect of the messenger; bad talking of the messenger; backbiting of the messenger has resulted in curses of sickness, spiritual stagnation, and spiritual retardation (instead of good health, spiritual growth, and advancement). Why? Because you cannot bite the hand that feeds you! It is sinful, blatant evil to speak ill of a servant of God who ministers to your spiritual needs. But don't take my word for it. Let us look at Numbers 12:1–15. The scripture reads:

And Miriam and Aaron spake against Moses because of the Ethiopian woman whom he had married: for he had married an Ethiopian woman. And they said, Hath the Lord indeed spoken only by Moses? hath he not spoken also by us? And the Lord heard it. (Now the man Moses was very meek, above all the men which were upon the face of the earth.) And the Lord spake suddenly unto Moses, and unto Aaron, and unto Miriam, Come out ye three unto the tabernacle of the congregation. And they three came out. And the Lord came down in the pillar of the cloud, and stood in the door of

Chapter Two

the tabernacle, and called Aaron and Miriam: and they both came forth. And he said, Hear now my words: If there be a prophet among you, I the Lord will make myself known unto him in a vision, and will speak unto him in a dream. My servant Moses is not so, who is faithful in all mine house. With him will I speak mouth to mouth, even apparently, and not in dark speeches; and the similitude of the Lord shall he behold: wherefore then were ye not afraid to speak against my servant Moses? And the anger of the Lord was kindled against them; and he departed. And the cloud departed from off the tabernacle; and, behold, Miriam became leprous, white as snow: and Aaron looked upon Miriam, and, behold, she was leprous. And Aaron said unto Moses, Alas, my lord, I beseech thee, lay not the sin upon us, wherein we have done foolishly, and wherein we have sinned. Let her not be as one dead, of whom the flesh is half consumed when he cometh out of his mother's womb. And Moses cried unto the Lord, saying, Heal her now, O God, I beseech thee. And the Lord said unto Moses, If her father had but spit in her face, should she not be ashamed seven days? let her be shut out from the camp seven days, and after that let her be received in again. And Miriam was shut out from the camp seven days: and the people journeyed not till Miriam was brought in again." (Num. 12:1–15 KJV).

God has not changed; those who speak against God's servants bring a curse on themselves. There may be various individuals in your congregation who the Lord could choose to deliver His Word. During the course of time, God can use anyone of these to relay His message to us. If we are to benefit from the Word and be able to move forward to serve God with excellence, we must receive His messengers with respect and humility. After all, 2 Chronicles 20:20b reminds us: "Believe in the Lord your God, so shall ye be established; believe his prophets, so shall ye prosper" (2 Chron. 20:20 KJV).

This leads me to two thoughts.

Thought 1: *The minister of God is chosen to proclaim the Word of God to the people of God.* The minister is not of his own. This is the very purpose for which he is called: to be the messenger of God, to proclaim the Word of God. Jesus to His messengers said:

> Go ye into all the world, and preach the gospel to every creature. (Mark 16:15)

> Ye have not chosen me, but I have chosen you, and ordained you, that ye should go and bring forth fruit, and that your fruit should remain: that whatsoever ye shall ask of the Father in my name, he may give it you. (John 15:16)

God warns the messenger:

> Take heed therefore unto yourselves, and to all the flock, over the which the Holy Ghost hath made you overseers, to feed the church of God, which he hath purchased with his own blood. (Acts 20:28)

> Feed the flock of God which is among you, taking the oversight thereof, not by constraint, but willingly; not for filthy lucre, but of a ready mind. (1 Pet. 5:2)

I have set watchmen upon thy walls, O Jerusalem, which shall never hold their peace day nor night: ye that make mention of the Lord, keep not silence. (Isa. 62:6)

And I will give you pastors according to mine heart, which shall feed you with knowledge and understanding. (Jer. 3:15)

And I will set up shepherds over them which shall feed them: and they shall fear no more, nor be dismayed, neither shall they be lacking, saith the Lord. (Jer. 23:4)

Son of man, I have made thee a watchman unto the house of Israel: therefore hear the word at my mouth, and give them warning from me. (Ezek. 3:17)

Note that the messenger has a great responsibility to God. If he/she is not functioning as God wants, your responsibility is to pray for him/her, but don't endanger your life and soul by talking against the messenger of God. This is sinful. This is evil. This is wrong. This will prevent you from moving forward in your life.

Thought 2: *Moses stood between God and the people*. He stood as the messenger of God. As the messenger of God, Moses is a picture of Christ. He acted as an intercessor. Jesus Christ came to earth as the perfect messenger of God to save man and to proclaim the way of salvation to man. His coming to earth was an angelic herald. "For unto you is born this day in the city of David a Saviour, which is Christ the Lord" (Luke 2:11).

His mission was made clear.

> For the Son of man is come to seek and to save that which was lost. (Luke 19:10)

> For God so loved the world, that he gave his only begotten Son, that whosoever believeth in him should not perish, but have everlasting life. For God sent not his Son into the world to condemn the world; but that the world through him might be saved. (John 3:16–17)

> Jesus saith unto him, I am the way, the truth, and the life: no man cometh unto the Father, but by me. (John 14:6)

> Him hath God exalted with his right hand to be a Prince and a Saviour, for to give repentance to Israel, and forgiveness of sins. (Acts 5:31)

> Wherefore he is able also to save them to the uttermost that come unto God by him, seeing he ever liveth to make intercession for them. (Heb. 7:25)

By being Messengers of God, we also accept the responsibility of being representatives of Christ. This means that we are challenged to live righteously. We are challenged to live holy! May the Lord help us! W*e allow the Word to shape us by* being receptive of God's messengers.

Further, we allow the Word to shape us by:

B. Getting Hungry to Receive from God

When the messenger delivers the message, the hearers must be anxiously prepared to receive it. Scripture reminds us: "Blessed are they which do hunger and thirst after righteousness: for they shall be filled" (Matt. 5:6 KJV). This means, among other things, that effort must be made to prepare the soil of our hearts to receive God's Word. How? By praying and worshipping, and creating a spiritual atmosphere to receive the Word, by being deliberate in avoiding distractions, and by taking notes for later review.

There has to be a hungering (a great desire to feast on God's Word) if we are to move forward in this season. We must develop and expand our spiritual appetite if we would benefit from the Word this year. We would have to ask God to increase our spiritual desires if we are to benefit from His Word and His messages this year. In this season, we can no longer show interest in our services based on who is speaking or teaching—may God help us! Rather, God is calling us to be spiritually receptive and discerning to glean from what He is saying to us through His chosen messengers.

The recipients of the messages were the Israelites, the people chosen by God to be His witnesses upon earth. As the people of God, Israel was a symbol of believers, a symbol of all who would become true followers of the Promised Seed, the coming Messiah and Savior of the world, the Lord Jesus Christ, God's very own Son. Note that Moses preached to all the Israelites, not just to a small number of them. These messages were so important that everyone needed to hear what was being preached.

Here is a thought: *The message of God's Word is so important that every person needs to hear and heed what God has to say.* People should be running to hear the Word of God preached and taught, seeking after the Lord while He may be found.

Seek ye the Lord while he may be found, call ye upon him while he is near. (Isa. 55:6)

Search the scriptures; for in them ye think ye have eternal life: and they are they which testify of me. (John 5:39)

But these are written, that ye might believe that Jesus is the Christ, the Son of God; and that believing ye might have life through his name. (John 20:31)

Chapter Two

For whatsoever things were written aforetime were written for our learning, that we through patience and comfort of the scriptures might have hope. (Rom. 15:4)

Study to show thyself approved unto God, a workman that needeth not to be ashamed, rightly dividing the word of truth. (2 Tim. 2:15)

All scripture is given by inspiration of God, and is profitable for doctrine, for reproof, for correction, for instruction in righteousness. (2 Tim. 3:16)

As newborn babes, desire the sincere milk of the word, that ye may grow thereby: If so be ye have tasted that the Lord is gracious. (1 Pet. 2:2–3)

These things have I written unto you that believe on the name of the Son of God; that ye may know that ye have eternal life, and that ye may believe on the name of the Son of God. (1 John 5:13)

Here is another thought: *The true Israelite believers were a type, a picture of all who would believe and become followers of the Promised Seed, the coming Messiah and Savior of the world, the Lord Jesus Christ.*

These early believers were examples for us to learn from. Speaking of our spiritual father, Abraham, the Bible said:

He staggered not at the promise of God through unbelief; but was strong in faith, giving glory to God; And being fully persuaded that, what he had promised, he was able also to perform. And therefore it was imputed to him for righteousness. Now it was not written for his sake alone, that it was imputed to him; But for us also, to whom it shall be imputed, if we believe on him that raised up Jesus our Lord from the dead; Who was delivered for our offences, and was raised again for our justification. (Rom. 4:20–25)

We are blessed to have in the Word the good as well as the bad examples of those who lived before us. We should be better off because of this.

Conclusion

And so, I close with two questions. —What preparations are you making this year to allow the Word of God to shape your life? Are you doing anything different from last year? In our endeavors to move forward in this era, we must allow the Word of God to shape us. This also means that we must be receptive and respectful of the messenger of the Word. And this simple change in attitude is necessary to crossover into a new spiritual dimension as discussed in the next chapter.

Chapter Three

Move Forward: Crossover!

"The Lord our God spake unto us in Horeb, saying, Ye have dwelt long enough in this mount" (Deut. 1:6 KJV).

Confession: *If I am to move forward this year and possess my Promised Land, I must cross over my Jordan! It is time to cross over!*

Introduction

At the time this Word came to Moses, Israel was camped by the river, right across from the great city of Jericho—poised to enter the Promised Land.

The people were anxious and excited. For years they had longed for this day to come, the day they would enter the Promised Land and be able to settle down, build their homes and cities, plant their crops, start their businesses, establish their worship center, and live like God expected them to live—in spiritual conquest and rest. They had never known what it was to have a permanent roof over their heads, to live in freedom and security, or to possess the spiritual peace and rest that God alone gives to those who walk obediently before Him. But now, at last, the Israelites stood at the threshold of laying claim to the inheritance promised by God. There the land lay, right across the river from them. Obviously, as any of us would do, various groups of Israelite believers often gathered on the bank of the Jordan River, excitedly talking about what they were going to do when they inherited their place in the Promised Land of God. This was the setting for the three great messages that are preached in the book of Deuteronomy, and this was the place where the Word of the Lord came to the people saying, "Ye have dwelt long enough in this mount: turn and take your journey and go."

After all, the people were settled by the Jordan River just across from the great city of Jericho. The people seemed just about ready to enter the

Chapter Three

Promised Land of God. But they needed to cross over! They seemed so close yet were so far.

I can't help painting a picture of the existing circumstances at the time. At last, the Israelites were that close, standing next to the Jordan River and a short distance away from entering the Promised Land of God. For generations—in fact, since their birth as a people (through Abraham)—the Israelites had been either slaves or pilgrims wandering about the face of the earth. They had no permanent home, no place to call their own. They had been slaves in Egypt for about 400 years, and mere pilgrims, sojourners—as foreigners moving about from place to place. They never owned land upon which they could build permanent homes, establish settled families and businesses, grow crops, and carry on commerce—not in a permanent, settled environment. They never knew rest. They were always having to break camp, move on, and then set up camp—over and over, again and again. They were never able to settle down and experience rest from wandering about. But despite this—in the face of their being mere pilgrims and sojourners upon earth—the Israelites had one great asset: hope. They had the hope of the Promised Land. You see, God had promised to give His dear people a great inheritance, the inheritance of a permanent home: the Promised Land, itself. And now, that glorious day of inheritance was rapidly approaching. Their glorious hope was about to be fulfilled. But this hope had to be activated by some action. They had to cross over!

It had been forty years since Moses had delivered the Israelites from Egyptian slavery, forty long, hard years of wandering about in the desert wilderness. And Moses had just died. They were so close, but they still needed to cross over!

Many of you have been like the Israelites—you wandered through the hardships of life for years. You fought countless battles with people, countless battles with sickness, countless battles of financial challenges, countless battles of family misunderstandings, countless battles of being falsely accused, battles of being taken for granted, battles of being abused and misused, and countless battles of various stresses. Many of you are now qualified to affirm that you have been through grave dangers, many toils, and many snares. You have seen the hand of God miraculously fighting for you, delivering you from the hand of the enemy.

But despite the challenges, despite the pains, you still haven't attained that satisfaction you crave; you still have not attained that goal, that desired result for which you struggled. Why? Because there is this one thing that you need to do to get your victory! There is just this one step you need to take to get your freedom. Just one thing, just one social effort, you need to undertake to set things straight. Just one action of obedience is required to realize your dream. This one step is necessary to step into your Promised Land! But today I want you to know that this is your year! This is your time! This season has been ordained for you to achieve it, to attain it, to fulfill it, to achieve it! This is the season that you need to cross over!

Come on, let your faith arise: Tell somebody, "cross over"! Cross over your Jordan! Cross over! Cross over your fears! Cross over the negative feelings! Cross over your negative speaking! Cross over your self-imposed barriers! Get yourself out of your way! Cross over people's negative labels of you! Cross over people's low expectations of you! Cross over your procrastination! Cross over your pride! Cross over! Cross over! Cross over! Cross over your Jordan! Enter into your Promised Land! For you have dwelt long enough in this mount! Tell somebody, "cross over"!

In considering the need to *cross over,* two strong lessons seem to be true:

(1) Some people stand on the threshold of receiving Christ and inheriting the Promised Land of God. But they have not yet crossed the threshold.

They were convicted and almost surrendered their lives to God. But they are still on the outside, still refusing to receive Christ as their Savior. The consequence is tragic: they continue to live in unbelief. They haven't received the promised gift of salvation and the prospect of heaven, they haven't known the spiritual conquest nor the rest that God provides for their souls, and have not inherited eternal life. They are still standing on the outskirts of the provisions God has made for us to be free from sin. They are still living dangerously on the edge of eternal damnation. But today God is saying, Cross over! Take that step of faith. Cross over! Surrender your life to Christ! Do it today! Do it now! Cross over!

"Wherefore (as the Holy Ghost saith), today if ye will hear his voice, Harden not your hearts" (Heb. 3:7–11).

(2) There are some believers who are on the threshold of entering the Promised Land of conquest, spiritual victory, and spiritual rest. But they have not yet crossed over the threshold.

After their conversion, they failed to study and grow in Christ and failed to learn how to walk and live for Christ. Some sin, some worldliness, some unbelief has seeped into their lives. Some sin that so easily besets us. The consequence is tragic: they live defeated instead of victorious lives, restless not restful lives. They simply do not experience spiritual conquest and victory, and do not possess the spiritual rest of their soul that conquers all the trials and temptations of this life. They fail to allow the peace of God that fills the soul to possess them and so experience the deepest sense of fulfillment, purpose, and satisfaction.

They know that the Lord said: "Take my yoke upon you, and learn of me; for I am meek and lowly in heart: and ye shall find rest unto your souls" (Matt. 11:29). But they struggle to do this and to live a life of victory. They understand that: "There hath no temptation taken you but such as is common to man: but God is faithful, who will not suffer you to be tempted above that ye are able; but will with the temptation also make a way to escape, that ye may be able to bear it" (1 Cor. 10:13). But they still find themselves trapped in a cat-and-mouse game of sinning and repenting, unable to enjoy the presence and power of God. But if I am describing you, today is your breakthrough! Today you break free! Today you make that change! Today you cross over! Today you cross over that Jordan that has been separating you from your promised victory and blessings of God. Your freedom awaits! Your blessings await! You must push yourself pass Jordan! Cross over!

Conclusion

As I close this chapter, let us look at some scripture verses. Scripture warns us:

> Let us therefore fear, lest, a promise being left us of entering into his rest, any of you should seem to come short of it. (Heb. 4:1)

> Let us labour therefore to enter into that rest, lest any man fall after the same example of unbelief. (Heb. 4:11)

> Submit yourselves therefore to God. Resist the devil, and he will flee from you. (James 4:7)

> For whatsoever is born of God overcometh the world: and this is the victory that overcometh the world, even our faith. Who is he that overcometh the world, but he that believeth that Jesus is the Son of God? (1 John 5:4–5)

If you are born of God, you are an overcomer; and you are well able to cross over your Jordan and possess your Promised Land.

Chapter Four

Move Forward with Hope

"The Lord our God spake unto us in Horeb, saying, Ye have dwelt long enough in this mount" (Deut. 1:6 KJV).

Confession: *I won't lose my hope in God! By faith, I move forward with it!*

Introduction

Hope is one of the most powerful forces on earth. It is a feeling of expectation and desire for a particular thing to happen. Hope is what keeps us going and what drives us to do more and more. Hope is the energy of life, the driving force that arouses a person to get up and march forth even in the face of hurt, disappointment, and defeat. Hope is the energy that drives us to achieve, accomplish, grow, develop, progress, and move forward! In fact, hope is what causes us to gather each morning for worship, trusting in a mighty God who brought us through last year, to bring us through again! Hope is that strong belief that resonates within us, giving us the assurance that He, who has done it in the past is well able to do it again, although this is a new year! Hope is a fascinating thing! Hope is that drive that takes us through a difficult night and helps us to yearn for the dawn of a new day. Hope is what helps us to understand and appreciate that "weeping may endure for a night but joy comes in the morning"! (Ps. 30:5). It is what keeps us while we look for the morning! In a challenging world, hope in God is that dynamism that keeps us looking forward for a brighter day and a better way. In fact, Romans 5:5 speaks of "[a] hope [that] maketh not ashamed." It is a hope that is an anchor for the soul—an energy, a strong feeling of certainty that amidst hardships, difficulties, criticisms, and sufferings, life will be sweeter someday! It was what kept Dr. Martin Luther King, Jr. marching fearlessly for human rights, even in the face of death.

It was what kept Nelson Mandela for years, waking up day after day in a South African prison cell in pursuit of justice and liberty for the oppressed. It was what energized James Ronald Webster to push for a better life for the people of Anguilla when so much opposition was dangerously stacked against him. It was what caused Jesus to make such a difficult journey toward Calvary, even when forsaken by His closest friends and followers.

Hope is that strong feeling, way down within our souls that brings comfort and reassurance to us that despite the challenges, despite the tests, one day, when this life is over, we'll fly away! Hope helps us see far beyond the here and now. It makes us sing when things aren't lovely and pray when things aren't holy. And everyone who has this hope in God, purifies himself (1 John 3:3 KJV).

Israel had hope — great hope — in the Promised Land of God. The great task that confronted Moses was how to keep this hope alive, how to keep it beating in the hearts of God's people. The great task that confronts Christian leaders everywhere in this end time is how do we keep hope alive in the hearts of God's people? What can we do to keep people spiritually focused? What can we do to keep people living lives of great expectancy because of the hope we have in Christ?

Keep this fact in mind: This passage is a sermon that Moses was preaching to the second generation of believers. Moses was doing all he could to arouse strong hope in the hearts of the people. If they were gripped by strong hope, they would courageously march into the Promised Land and lay claim of their inheritance. They would allow nothing to stop them. Knowing this, Moses challenged the second generation to remember the experience of their parents: how they had started out with such great hope, but how miserably they had failed.

We must learn from those who have gone on before us! After all, Romans 15:4 teaches us: "For whatsoever things were written aforetime were written for our learning, that we through patience and comfort of the scriptures might have hope" (Rom. 15:4 KJV).

The New International version puts it this way: "For everything that was written in the past was written to teach us, so that through the endurance taught in the Scriptures and the encouragement they provide we might have hope" (Rom. 15:4 NIV). And so, our hope is grounded in our experiences but especially in our memories. When we remember what God has done for us, when we remember where God brought us from, when we remember how God delivered us in the past, our faith and hope in Him increases, and we are able to face new challenges with a fresh and confident perspective. This seemed to be the situation that existed in our text. In keeping hope alive, Moses challenged the Israelites to:

1. Remember your call and charge from God (Deut. 1:6–8).

Moses was reminding the people of the call and charge of God to break camp and leave Sinai. He was inspiring them to move on—march and lay claim to the Promised Land. This is a picture of our marching to heaven, and of spiritual conquest and rest to be gained from attaining it. In 1:6–8, the text reads:

The Lord our God spake unto us in Horeb, saying, Ye have dwelt long enough in this mount: Turn you, and take your journey, and go to the mount of the Amorites, and unto all the places nigh thereunto, in the plain, in the hills, and in the vale, and in the south, and by the sea side, to the land of the Canaanites, and unto Lebanon, unto the great river, the river Euphrates. Behold, I have set the land before you: go in and possess the land which the Lord sware unto your fathers, Abraham, Isaac, and Jacob, to give unto them and to their seed after them. (Deut. 1:6–8 KJV)

This was a call from complacency, that feeling of just being satisfied. This was a call to action. This was a call to spiritual progress and spiritual expansion. Horeb was the mountain range in which Mt. Sinai was located. Because of this, Mt. Sinai is sometimes called Mt. Horeb (Exod. 3:1; 17:6; 33:6; 1 Kings. 19:8; Ps. 106:19; Mal. 4:4). It is interesting to note that the word *Horeb* means desolate or desolation—complete loneliness, unhappiness, emptiness. This means that the Israelites were camped at a place of desolation for long enough. In fact, the Israelites had been camped at Horeb, or Mt. Sinai, for about a year when the charge of God to break camp was given. God charged His people to leave Sinai—to march and lay claim to the Promised Land of God.

The Israelites were camped at one place for too long. They had become comfortable, settled, and satisfied. They had failed to grow, failed to develop, and failed to advance in their journey with the Lord. They had lost sight of the hope that had propelled them forward in the past. Don't lose sight of the hope that propels you on your Christian journey. Don't lose sight of the promises of God for your life! Don't lose sight of the Promised Land! Don't ever forget that this world is not our home; we are on a journey to heaven. Scripture challenges us to keep hope alive. The Word tells us: "Happy is he that hath the God of Jacob for his help, whose hope is in the Lord his God" (Ps. 146:5 KJV).

In his time of discouragement, David rekindled his hope. He questioned: "Why art thou cast down, O my soul? and why art thou disquieted within me? hope in God: for I shall yet praise him, who is the health of my countenance, and my God" (Ps. 43:5 KJV).

Paul understood the need for the Christian hope. In Romans 15:13, he affirmed: "Now the God of hope fill you with all joy and peace in believing, that ye may abound in hope, through the power of the Holy Ghost" (Rom. 15:13 KJV). On our journey to the Promised Land, God wants us to abound in hope, through the power of the Holy Ghost!

Years ago, Robert Critchley wrote with great assurance:

> My hope is built on nothing less
> Than Jesus' blood and righteousness
> I dare not trust the sweetest frame
> But wholly lean on Jesus' name
>
> ***On Christ the solid Rock I stand***
> ***All other ground is sinking sand***
> ***All other ground is sinking sand***
>
> When darkness hides His lovely face
> I rest on His unchanging grace
> In every high and stormy gale

Chapter Four

My anchor holds within the veil

On Christ the solid Rock I stand
All other ground is sinking sand
All other ground is sinking sand

(https://www.musixmatch.com)

Our hope is in Christ!

Losing hope in God will cause us to become stagnant, settled, and satisfied. Losing hope in God will cause us to lose spiritual zeal, fervor, and motivation to go on. Ephesians 2:11–22 makes the point:

Wherefore remember, that ye being in time past Gentiles in the flesh, who are called Uncircumcision by that which is called the Circumcision in the flesh made by hands;

That at that time ye were without Christ, being aliens from the commonwealth of Israel, and strangers from the covenants of promise, having no hope, and without God in the world:

But now in Christ Jesus ye who sometimes were far off are made nigh by the blood of Christ.

For he is our peace, who hath made both one, and hath broken down the middle wall of partition between us;

Having abolished in his flesh the enmity, even the law of commandments contained in ordinances; for to make in himself of twain one new man, so making peace;

And that he might reconcile both unto God in one body by the cross, having slain the enmity thereby:

And came and preached peace to you which were afar off, and to them that were nigh.

For through him we both have access by one Spirit unto the Father.

Now therefore ye are no more strangers and foreigners, but fellowcitizens with the saints, and of the household of God; And are built upon the foundation of the apostles and prophets, Jesus Christ himself being the chief corner stone;

In whom all the building fitly framed together groweth unto an holy temple in the Lord: In whom ye also are builded together for an habitation of God through the Spirit. (Ephesians 2:11–22 KJV)

Our hope is in Christ! – A solid and firm foundation!

We must remember the call and charge of God to break free from the camp of desolation, leave Sinai (that place where we received our instructions), and move on, marching forward to lay claim on the Promised Land. Tell somebody: "Keep hope alive!"

2. Remember the terrible sins that kept the first generation of Israelites out of the Promised Land (Deut. 1:18–39).

The presence of sin in our lives will keep us from moving forward and attaining God's promises for us as His people. Sins of fear, unbelief, grumbling, and rebellion will disqualify us from attaining to the spiritual stature and standards that God has ordained for us. Let us not lose sight of the fact that the messages of Deuteronomy were preached forty years after the Exodus of Israel from Egyptian slavery. Keep in mind that Egypt is a symbol of the world with all its enslavements and bondages. The Exodus (the movement of God's people from Egypt) is a picture of God's great deliverance from the enslavement of this world, from the sin and death of this world.

Standing there on the banks of the Jordan River, the people must have thought about the great Exodus that had taken place forty years earlier; and remembered the forty years of wilderness wanderings that had just ended. This is significant: it means that the people standing before Moses were the children of the Israelites who had experienced the great Exodus and the giving of the law at Mt. Sinai. Remember, all the adults of the first generation—twenty years old and older—had died in the desert wilderness; because of their terrible sin and unbelief, they had died under the judgment of God. Only the children twenty years old and younger had survived the ordeal of the wilderness wanderings and God's judgment. Many of the second generation had not yet been born or were too young to understand the law of God when it was first taught at Mt. Sinai. Consequently, there was a great need for the present generation to be reminded before they could enter the Promised Land of God. In fact, the second generation needed a special reminder since they had not been eyewitnesses of the events of God's glorious power in the delivering and guiding of God's people. There was a dire need for these events to be reviewed one last time before the present generation of believers launched their campaign to claim the promised inheritance.

Similarly, I feel that there is a dire need for this present generation to be reminded of God's standards for entrance into His Promised Land. A fresh grasp and consciousness of God's power and guidance were needed then, and a fresh grasp and consciousness of God's power is needed now. The people needed a new work of God's Spirit in their hearts and lives then. And I dare say that we all need a new work of God's Spirit in our hearts and lives now. The people needed to be reminded that sins of fear, unbelief, grumbling, and rebellion will bring death—spiritual and physical death. And we also need to be reminded that sins of fear, unbelief, grumbling, and rebellion will bring death—spiritual and physical death! These sins will destroy the hope you have in Christ and should never be allowed to germinate in our hearts.

Even in difficulties, we must refuse to give up our hope. We must be reminded that Isaiah 40:31 (NIV) says: "But those who hope in the Lord will renew their strength. They will soar on wings like eagles; they will run and not grow weary, they will walk and not faint."

Conclusion

And so, what am I saying? I want to encourage that amidst your tests, amidst your hardships, and amidst the various distractions of life, hold on to your hope! Hold on to your faith! Hold on to your trust! Hold on to your God! He is still the hope for what's happening in the world. Move forward but do so with hope! Even in the face of COVID-19, He is our hope for healing.

Chapter Five

Move Forward: Look to Jesus for Healing

"The Lord our God spake unto us in Horeb, saying, Ye have dwelt long enough in this mount" (Deut. 1:6 KJV).

When the Canaanite king of Arad, who lived in the Negev, heard that Israel was coming along the road to Atharim, he attacked the Israelites and captured some of them. Then Israel made this vow to the Lord: "If you will deliver these people into our hands, we will totally destroy their cities." The Lord listened to Israel's plea and gave the Canaanites over to them. They completely destroyed them and their towns; so the place was named Hormah. They traveled from Mount Hor along the route to the Red Sea, to go around Edom. But the people grew impatient on the way; they spoke against God and against Moses, and said, "Why have you brought us up out of Egypt to die in the wilderness? There is no bread! There is no water! And we detest this miserable food!" Then the Lord sent venomous snakes among them; they bit the people and many Israelites died. The people came to Moses and said, "We sinned when we spoke against the Lord and against you. Pray that the Lord will take the snakes away from us." So Moses prayed for the people. The Lord said to Moses, "Make a snake and put it up on a pole; anyone who is bitten can look at it and live." So Moses made a bronze snake and put it up on a pole. Then when anyone was bitten by a snake and looked at the bronze snake, they lived. (Num. 21:1–9 NIV).

Confession: *Declare with conviction: Jesus has the power to heal me, so I now look to Him and I am perfectly whole!*

Introduction

Marching in the wilderness was hard and difficult. At the end of each day, the people were bound to be tired, exhausted, and bone-weary. This passage shows how fatigue and exhaustion got to the people, how they had become so bone-weary that they lapsed back into their grumbling and unbelief. They began once again to attack God and His dear servant. The Scripture and the following outline clearly paint the picture.

a. Note the tragic situation: the people had to bypass or detour around Edom (vv. 4–5).

This was a long distance out of the way. In Numbers 20:14 and following, Moses had sent two diplomatic letters to the king of Edom, asking permission to pass through their land. The king had rejected the appeal and had even gone so far as to threaten attack against the Israelites. Therefore, Moses had to lead the people on a detour around the land of Edom. As stated, this was a long distance out of the way for the people to travel. Fatigue and exhaustion set in, and they grew impatient. They began to grumble and murmur against God and against Moses.

Don't let fatigue and exhaustion beset you on your spiritual journey to the point that you become mischievous and unproductive in the kingdom of God! Some of you have been on a long journey, and you have experienced various tests and hardships along the way. But you must continue to believe; you must continue to trust; you must continue to affirm that the toils of the road would seem nothing when you get to the end of the way.

We must note the admonition of the apostle Paul to the Galatians: "And let us not be weary in well doing: for in due season we shall reap, if we faint not" (Gal. 6:9 KJV).

Fatigue and exhaustion set in, and they grew impatient. They began to grumble and murmur against God and against Moses. They asked why they had been led out of Egypt into the desert wilderness to die: there was no bread and no water in the desert wilderness. They expressed their dissatisfaction with the "worthless manna." Remember that the manna was the bread from heaven, the bread that God, Himself had provided to feed the people through their wilderness wanderings. Ungratefulness was setting in.

Chapter Five

We must understand that even in our difficult moments, we can't afford to become ungrateful and despise the provisions of God. In the original text, the word the people used to describe the manna means "contemptible, worthless bread"; it means miserable, wretched, despicable, cheap bread. It even has the idea of cursing the heavenly bread, the bread that had been provided by God, Himself. The people had constantly grumbled about God's gracious provision during their forty-year wilderness wandering, but this time it was different. They actually stated that they detested the manna, and they cursed it. It was despicable and worthless; at best they saw it as junk food. This time, the people had gone too far. God had no choice but to judge and chastise them, and to do so severely. We must be careful that our grumblings, complaining, and unthankfulness do not bring God's chastisement on our lives.

b. Note the judgment, the chastisement of the Lord: He sent snakes among them, and many of them died (v. 6).

The King James Version describes them as "fiery serpents," that is, poisonous snakes. The poison was obviously strong, very potent—the kind of venom that causes a horrible, agonizing death. This is indicated by the fact that many of the people subsequently died.

Let us not miss the point here, those believers who grumble and complain against God and His leaders are judged severely by God; and some even died! The attack by snakes is symbolic of the attacks of the enemy. The enemy is often depicted as a snake. God exposed the Israelites to evil. He rid them of His protection so that they were attacked by the enemy. Disobedience and rebellion against God's commands exposes us to attacks from the enemy, and to spiritual and physical death. Yet those who find themselves in a state of rebellion or disobedience can confess and repent before it is too late.

c. Note the Confession and repentance of the people: they confessed their sin and asked Moses to pray for them, asking God to take away the snakes (v. 7).

This Moses did. He was the servant of God, so he once again forgave them for their attacks against him and the Lord. As their minister, he loved them, so he again became their intercessor and mediator before God. No doubt, he begged God to forgive the sin of the people and to have mercy upon them.

Sin cannot be glossed over. Sin cannot be covered. It has to be confessed; it has to be forgiven. We cannot keep sinning and just moving on. "If we confess our sins, [God] is faithful and just to forgive us of our sins and cleanse us from all unrighteousness" (1 John 1:9). But sin has to be confessed! The Israelites confessed their sins and sought repentance.

d. Note the surprising answer of the Lord (v. 8).

The Lord told Moses to make a replica of a snake and hang it on a high pole. Then

God spelled out a condition for deliverance and healing: a person had to look at the snake hanging upon the pole. If he looked, he would be healed and would live.

Over 2000 years ago, God through Jesus, spelled out a condition for deliverance and healing. This is one of the great symbols of Jesus Christ in the Scripture—His being hung upon the cross for the sins of the world. This is exactly what Christ said:

> And as Moses lifted up the serpent in the wilderness, even so must the Son of man be lifted up: That whosoever believeth in him should not perish, but have eternal life. For God so loved the world, that he gave his only begotten Son, that whosoever believeth in him should not perish, but have everlasting life. (John 3:14–16)

This is still God's answer to all those who confess their sins and repent.

Jesus is still the answer and the provision for all sickness and sin! He is still able to heal all manner of sicknesses and diseases for those who trust in Him.

e. Note the obedience of Moses: he hung a bronze snake on a pole just as instructed by God (v. 9).

The people were delivered, but only some. Only those who looked at the snake and believed the promise of God lived (v. 9). Keep in mind, this is a picture of deliverance by looking at (believing in) the cross of Jesus Christ (John 3:14–15).

I want to assure someone: somebody who has suffered for years, somebody who has received bad news from a doctor, or somebody who has been given a bad diagnosis. Also, I would assure somebody who has to be constantly medicated, or somebody who has tested positive for the coronavirus, including somebody who has settled for a condition, a sickness, a disease—Jesus is still the answer!

Jesus is still the Healer! Jesus is still the Deliverer! Jesus is still the Redeemer! And all He wants us to do is to look to Him! The bronze snake is a picture of unbelief, but it is also a symbol of Christ the Savior.

So, let me conclude with three summary thoughts:

(1) Jesus Christ is the manna, the bread from heaven.

God has given Jesus Christ to feed the souls of people. People hunger and crave for the food of purpose, meaning, and significance in life. Christ and Christ alone can meet the hunger of the human soul. Jesus Christ is the Bread of Life. Jesus affirmed this in John 6:48–51:

> I am that bread of life. Your fathers did eat manna in the wilderness, and are dead. This is the bread which cometh down from heaven, that a man may eat thereof, and not die. I am the living bread which came down from heaven: if any man eat of this bread, he shall live forever: and the bread that I will give is my flesh, which I will give for the life of the world. (John 6:48–51)

> This is that bread which came down from heaven: not as your fathers did eat manna, and are dead: he that eateth of this bread shall live forever. (John 6:58)

(2) The Israelites cursed the bread of God, which was a symbol of Jesus Christ.

Any person who curses Jesus Christ will be severely judged by God. Any person who looks upon Jesus Christ as contemptible, worthless, wretched—as being useless—is going to face the wrath of God, a judgment beyond comprehension.

> He that believeth on the Son hath everlasting life: and he that believeth not the Son shall not see life; but the wrath of God abideth on him. (John 3:36)

> For the wrath of God is revealed from heaven against all ungodliness and unrighteousness of men, who hold the truth in unrighteousness. (Rom. 1:18)

> The Lord knoweth how to deliver the godly out of temptations, and to reserve

the unjust unto the day of judgment to be punished. (2 Pet. 2:9)

(3) Jesus Christ has been lifted up as the Savior of the world.

God lifted up Christ just as the serpent was lifted up as a symbol of healing and deliverance. Any person who looks to Christ and believes in Him will be healed, saved, and delivered. The Word of God confirms:

> And as Moses lifted up the serpent in the wilderness, even so must the Son of man be lifted up: That whosoever believeth in him should not perish, but have eternal life. For God so loved the world, that he gave his only begotten Son, that whosoever believeth in him should not perish, but have everlasting life. (John 3:14–16)

> Verily, verily, I say unto you, He that heareth my word, and believeth on him that sent me, hath everlasting life, and

shall not come into condemnation; but is passed from death unto life. (John 5:24)

That if thou shalt confess with thy mouth the Lord Jesus, and shalt believe in thine heart that God hath raised him from the dead, thou shalt be saved. For with the heart man believeth unto righteousness; and with the mouth confession is made unto salvation. (Rom. 10:9–10)

Looking to Jesus can bring you deliverance and healing. Just as the people had to look toward the bronze serpent on a pole, today we must look to Jesus and the work He has done on the cross. For by His stripes, we were healed; and being healed spiritually, physically, and emotionally affords us the opportunity to serve with excellence. This is our emphasis for the next chapter.

Chapter Six

Move Forward: Serve with Excellence

The Lord our God spake unto us in Horeb, saying, Ye have dwelt long enough in this mount. (Deut. 1:6 KJV).

[They] were beyond measure astonished, saying, He hath done all things well: he maketh both the deaf to hear, and the dumb to speak. (Mark 7:37 KJV)

Be ye therefore followers of God, as dear children. (Eph. 5:1 KJV)

Confession: *We are serving an excellent God! Our great challenge is to be like Him!*

Introduction

We have been talking about moving forward. But if we are to move forward we must improve the quality of our service to the Lord. How do we serve the Lord? We serve the Lord when we serve our fellowman. This includes the service we render on our jobs or places of employment as well as the service we provide in ministry. Having being exposed to how quickly life can change, we must now challenge ourselves not to return to producing service as usual or service of mediocrity. Instead, we must move forward, serving with excellence! We must now work with the dexterity and enthusiasm that is typical of our final day. Indeed, our experiences have dictated that we are uncertain as to when this day would be; and so, we must cultivate a lifestyle that produces service of excellence.

But you may ask, why serve with excellence? Because the God we serve is excellent! This means that He is extremely good, outstandingly capable, and His power is beyond human comprehension. He is Jehovah, a God who is awesome in power; a God whose impressive qualities are beyond verbal descriptions. He is excellent!

The scriptures declare and affirm the excellencies of God. The heaven declares the glory (magnificence or excellence) of God, and the firmament shows His handy works. David in Psalm 8 emphatically declares:

O Lord our Lord, how excellent is thy name in all the earth! Who hast set thy glory above the heavens. Out of the mouth of babes and sucklings hast thou ordained strength because of thine enemies, that thou mightest still the enemy and the avenger. When I consider thy heavens, the work of thy fingers, the moon and the stars, which thou hast ordained; What is man, that thou art mindful of him? And the son of man, that thou visitest him? For thou hast made him a little lower than the angels, and hast crowned him with glory (magnificence / excellence) and honour. Thou madest him to have dominion over the works of thy hands; thou hast put all things under his feet: All sheep and oxen, yea, and the beasts of the field; The fowl of the air, and the fish of the sea, and whatsoever passeth through the paths of the seas. O

Lord our Lord, how excellent is thy name in all the earth! (Ps. 8:1–9 KJV)

The Lord and His name are one; and He is excellent! His every work is excellent! Can we praise Him for His mighty acts that are excellent?

Isaiah 12:5–6 KJV affirm this truth: "Sing unto the Lord; for he hath done excellent things: this is known in all the earth. Cry out and shout, thou inhabitant of Zion: for great is the Holy One of Israel in the midst of thee."

He is excellent! His name is excellent! His works are excellent! Could we exalt the great and holy one in the midst of us! Could we adore Him for His excellence?

Isaiah 28:28–29 tells of the excellent guidance of God. It reads: "Bread flour must be ground; Therefore he does not thresh it forever, Break it with his cartwheel, Or crush it with his horsemen. This also comes from the LORD of hosts, Who is wonderful in counsel and excellent in guidance" (Isa. 28:28–29 NKJV).

God is excellent in guidance! Job 37:23 tells of the excellent power, judgment and abundant justice of God. It reads: "As for the Almighty, we cannot find Him; He is excellent in power, In judgment and abundant justice; He does not oppress" (Job 37:23 NKJV).

God is excellent in so many ways; and our God, who is excellent, calls us to a life of excellence. He wants us to imitate Him in all we do. Put another way:

1. **We are called to exhibit excellence in all things.**

Mark 7 records many miraculous acts of Jesus during His earthly ministry. And one of the many great descriptions of Jesus comes from Mark 7:37 where it says "People were overwhelmed with amazement… 'He [Jesus] has done everything well.'"

As followers of Christ, this passage should give us great food for thought. As those seeking to imitate Jesus in every way imaginable, can we truly say we are doing *everything* well? Can we say we are doing *everything* with excellence at work, at church, on our jobs, and at home? The fact is that all of us have areas of our lives where we are falling short of Jesus's excellent standard. I think this is even more obvious today. Why? Because now more than ever, so many of us believe the lies that we have to do it all, be it all, and have it all. We are overcommitted, overwhelmed, and overstressed, making a millimeter of progress in a million directions because we fail to discern the essential from the nonessential in our work and in our homes. This is a recipe for mediocrity, not excellence, and I would argue the problem has spread throughout the Church today.

This is also an era when everybody is an expert. Have you noticed how everyone knows it all? Just because you can google every topic and receive some form of response doesn't mean that you are an expert on every subject. In fact, everything written online is not authentic or true.

And this fallacy is also prominent in the church. Why should we care? Because anything less than excellence falls short of the standard Christians have been called to.

In 1 Corinthians 10:31, Paul writes, "So whether you eat or drink or whatever you do, do it all for the glory of God." In other words, whatever you do, do it of a high standard, with high quality, high renown or honor; magnificence or great beauty; do it with excellence. The late founder of Evangelism Explosion, Dr. James Kennedy, paraphrased this passage and called his congregation to "excellence in all things and all things to God's glory." And this is the standard we are called to— "excellence in all things and all things to God's glory."

In light of the gracious mercies of God especially during this pandemic, there are many good reasons to pursue excellence in all things, especially in our chosen work. Excellence in our vocations advances our careers, makes us winsome to the world, grants us influence, and can lead to opportunities to share the gospel. But none of these good things should be the primary motivators for us as we pursue excellence in our work and the other roles God has called us to fulfill in our lives. We pursue excellence for a much more fundamental purpose—because excellence is how we best reflect the character of Christ, and to love and serve our neighbors as ourselves. In other words, excellence is our most everyday form of ministry. As we will understand later, it is through the ministry of excellence that we glorify God and love others well through our work. In the words of the apostle Paul: "Whether therefore ye eat, or drink, or whatsoever ye do, do all to the glory of God" (1 Cor. 10:31 KJV). God wants us to serve Him in excellence. This means that:

2. **We are challenged to forsake mediocrity.**

Because first of all, we were made in the image and likeness of the excellent God. Mediocrity does not represent an excellent God. Mediocrity comes from the word *mediocre*, which means of an average or low standard, not so good in quality. And mediocrity doesn't represent Jehovah God. In fact, mediocrity is a failure of true love. How? In Matthew 22:36–40, a young man came to Jesus and started a conversation that went like this:

Master, which is the great commandment in the law? Jesus said unto him, Thou shalt love the Lord thy God with all thy heart, and with all thy soul, and with all thy mind. This is the first and great commandment. And the second is like unto it, Thou shalt love thy neighbour as thyself. On these two commandments hang all the law and the prophets. (Matt. 22:36–40 KJV)

Note that when Jesus was asked what the greatest commandments were, he replied, "Love the Lord your God ... and ... Love your neighbor as yourself." Excellent work is one way in which we fulfill Jesus's command to love God by revealing His character of excellence to those around us. Excellence is also necessary for keeping the second commandment in our work. As believers, we can't say we are seeking to love our neighbor as ourselves and then do anything we do with mediocrity. Think of the extreme example of a Christian doctor. While that doctor may pray with her patients, share the gospel with her co-workers, and donate money to her church, her most basic form of ministry is in being an excellent doctor. If she were a mediocre medical professional, her patients' lives might be at risk. The doctor's first responsibility in her work ought to be the ministry of excellence—serving her patients as best she knows how, giving them the same level of care she would expect for herself and her family.

Now, for most of us, the relative skill of our work isn't going to mean the difference between life and death. But we all have an opportunity to obey Jesus's command to love our neighbors as ourselves by choosing to do excellent work and going far beyond the minimum standards required in our jobs. For, in Jesus's words: "for in as much as you have done it unto the least of these my brethren, you have done it unto Me." Matt Perman puts it this way:

Slack work is like vandalism because it makes life harder for people—just like vandalism. Christians are to be the opposite of vandals and slackers in their work. We are called to give God our best and give God our all. We are to do work that will truly benefit people by going the extra mile rather than just doing the minimum necessary. Excellence in our work is actually a form of generosity and love, and poor quality is a form of stinginess and selfishness. Shoddy work is not just shoddy work; it's a failure of love.

As Christians, we shouldn't seek to do the bare minimum in our jobs to collect a paycheck. If we believe our work is a calling from God, we will "work heartily, as working for the Lord" (Col. 3:23), seeking to glorify God and love others well by being the most focused and excellent workers we can possibly be. Excellence in our work isn't just a means to some personal gain. Excellence is our most fundamental form of ministry in our work. Let this truth encourage you to focus on pursuing mastery of your craft, becoming the most exceptional version of yourself for God's glory and the good of others. We are reminded: "And whatsoever ye do, do it heartily, as to the Lord, and not unto men" (Col. 3:23 KJV).

Finally:

3. We are called to proclaim the excellence of God.

What we do as individuals is no different than the purpose of our lives, which is to glorify God in everything we do (1 Cor. 10:31). We are called to be glory carriers. We carry the glory or excellence of God! Our behavior must reflect this. Our speech must reflect this. Our mannerisms must reflect this. The quality of our work must reflect this. We carry the glory of God. This means that our lives must glorify God. *Glorify* is a word that we use so much that it can be difficult to define. John Piper says, to glorify God simply means to "reflect his greatness" or reveal his character to others.

Jordan Raynor, author of the book: *Called to create*, argues that 'if the purpose of our work and living is to reveal the Lord's character to the world, what exactly are his characteristics? The Bible describes God in many ways, but it is his character of creative excellence that is perhaps most visible to us'. All of his handiwork is compelling evidence of His creative supremacy as the Creator of this world; and when considered, what is more fitting a description of His work than then the term: excellence! It is no wonder that Carl Boberg (1885), inspired by The Spirit exclaimed: "Then sings my soul, My Saviour God to Thee, how great Thou Art! How great Thou art!"

God's character of excellence also shone through in Jesus's life on earth, with his contemporaries marveling that "He has done everything well." How many things? Everything! He has done everything well! And His excellence must therefore be reflected in our worship. We worship the preeminent God who surpasses all others in power, authority and might—a perfect God!

Excellent is far too common a word to describe the God of this universe. But it is the closest we as mere mortals can hope to understand and attain. As God's children, we are called to be image bearers of our exceptional Father. In Ephesians 5:1, Paul instructs the Church "as beloved children" to "be imitators of God"—aspire to be like God. Commenting on this passage, theologian Andreas Köstenberger asks, "How should we respond to God's excellence? In short, we should seek to imitate and emulate it ... As God's redeemed children, we are to strive to be like God. This, it appears, includes striving for excellence."

John Piper puts it this way: "God created me—and you—to live with a single, all-embracing, all-transforming passion—namely, a passion to glorify God by enjoying and displaying his supreme excellence in all the spheres of life" (www.desiringgod.org). According to Raynor, "we glorify God when we imitate His character of excellence and in doing so "proclaim the excellencies of him who called you out of darkness into his marvelous light" (1 Pet. 2:9)(*The Ministry of Excellence*, us12.campaign-archive.com). After all, we live surrounded by darkness in a world that is desperate for something excellent and true. There is perhaps no more influential "sphere of life" for us to shine the light of Christ than in our chosen work. When we work with excellence, we have the great privilege of glorifying God and proclaiming his excellencies to the world around us. Why? For we are a peculiar people in relationship with a spectacular God. As 1 Peter puts it: "But ye are a chosen generation, a royal priesthood, an holy nation, a peculiar people; that ye should shew forth the praises of him who hath called you out of darkness into his marvellous light" (1 Pet. 2:9 KJV).

Conclusion

Well, what does all this mean? Understanding who God is changes our attitude of how we approach Him. Understanding who God is changes the way we worship Him. Understanding who God is changes our expectations of being in His presence. We now understand that He wants to astound us! We now appreciate that He can do the miraculous. He can save! He can heal! He can deliver! He can set free! He provides! He sustains! He is excellent! He is Savior! He is Redeemer! He is Sanctifier! He wants to heal you! He wants to help you! He is your answer! He is your Problem Solver! And He bids you come to Him right now. Why not draw closer to Him by faith? Come! Let the God of excellence meet you at the point of your need!

Chapter Seven

Move Forward: Get Under the Cloud of God!

"The Lord our God spake unto us in Horeb, saying, Ye have dwelt long enough in this mount" (Deut. 1:6 KJV).

And on the day that the tabernacle was reared up the cloud covered the tabernacle, namely, the tent of the testimony: and at even there was upon the tabernacle as it were the appearance of fire, until the morning.

So it was alway: the cloud covered it by day, and the appearance of fire by night.

And when the cloud was taken up from the tabernacle, then after that the children of Israel journeyed: and in the place where the cloud abode, there the children of Israel pitched their tents.

At the commandment of the Lord the children of Israel journeyed, and at the commandment of the Lord they pitched: as long as the cloud abode upon the tabernacle they rested in their tents.

And when the cloud tarried long upon the tabernacle many days, then the children of Israel kept the charge of the Lord, and journcyed not.

And so it was, when the cloud was a few days upon the tabernacle; according to the commandment of the Lord they abode in their tents, and according to the commandment of the Lord they journeyed.

And so it was, when the cloud abode from even unto the morning, and that the cloud was taken up in the morning, then they journeyed: whether it was by day or by night that the cloud was taken up, they journeyed.

Or whether it were two days, or a month, or a year, that the cloud tarried upon the tabernacle, remaining thereon, the children of Israel abode in their tents, and journeyed not: but when it was taken up, they journeyed.

At the commandment of the Lord they rested in the tents, and at the commandment of the Lord they journeyed: they kept the charge of the Lord, at the commandment of the Lord by the hand of Moses." (Num. 9:15–23 KJV)

Confession: *We need to get under the guidance, leadership, and influence of the Holy Ghost to steer us through this troubled world!*

Introduction

One of the awesome benefits of being in a relationship with Jehovah God is to be able to experience His constant guidance and leadership in your life. After all, this is one of the huge benefits of the covenant we have when we come to Christ. He who has called us to Himself wants to direct our lives aright. He wants to work everything out for our good. This is what He longs to do for all His children. He wants to guide us daily. He wants to guide us in the big things, and He wants to guide us in the little things. For as the scripture tells us, "For those who are led by the Spirit of God are the children of God" (Rom. 8:14 NIV). And so, in a world that is so troubled and chaotic, God's children need guidance.

After leaving Egypt, the children of Israel traveling through the wilderness places did not have this privilege though, for the Holy Ghost was not given as yet. There was instead, the provision of the fiery cloud, that is, the cloud that guided God's people throughout their wilderness wanderings. The cloud was a striking symbol of God's presence and guidance, for the God we serve, the Great Jehovah God, always makes a way to ensure that His will concerning our lives is fulfilled. When the children of Israel needed a deliverer, He provided Moses. When they needed to get through the Red Sea, He provided a dry pathway. When they needed food, He provided manna from heaven. When they needed water, He provided it from a rock. When they needed laws to live by, He provided the Ten Commandments on stones. When they needed direction in their travels, He provided for them a cloud. The Great Jehovah God has always made sure that His will concerning the lives of His children is fulfilled, and He still provides for all our needs today. He promised to "supply *all* our needs according to His riches in glory by Christ Jesus" (Phil. 4:19) Oh Lord! We ought to give Him glory! At a critical time, when God's people needed direction for their lives, He provided a cloud.

Note some truths from the Scripture:

1. The cloud came down and hovered above the Tabernacle right after the Tabernacle's dedication (Exod. 40:34–38).

The scripture reads:

> Then a cloud covered the tent of the congregation, and the glory of the Lord

filled the tabernacle. And Moses was not able to enter into the tent of the congregation, because the cloud abode thereon, and the glory of the Lord filled the tabernacle. And when the cloud was taken up from over the tabernacle, the children of Israel went onward in all their journeys: But if the cloud were not taken up, then they journeyed not till the day that it was taken up. For the cloud of the Lord was upon the tabernacle by day, and fire was on it by night, in the sight of all the house of Israel, throughout all their journeys. (Exod. 40:34–38 KJV

This shows at least two things: first, that God was concerned for the guidance of His children; and second, He provided guidance early for them on their pilgrim journey. God is concerned about our guidance. It is not His intention for us to fight life battles alone. He wants to lead and direct our lives aright. He wants to champion our affairs. He wants to be an integral part of our journey with Him. He doesn't want to leave us alone in our spiritual wilderness journey. In the words of this great hymn: "*No, Never alone, No, Never alone; He promised never to leave me, never to leave us alone*" (https://hymnary.org). And so, early in the journey of His children, He made provision for this. He provided a cloud.

2. The cloud changed its appearance at night - changed into a fiery cloud so the people could continue to see it (Num. 9:15–16).

These verses of our text read:

> And on the day that the tabernacle was reared up the cloud covered the tabernacle, namely, the tent of the testimony: and at even there was upon the tabernacle as it were the appearance of fire, until the morning. So it was always: the cloud covered it by day, and the appearance of fire by night.

This symbolized the continued, unbroken presence and guidance of the almighty God. My! My! He was there all the time through thick and thin, through good times and bad times. They may not had done everything to accommodate Him. They may not had done everything to entertain Him. But He was there all the time. Hovering above the Tabernacle by day and turning into a blazing fire by night— the cloud must have been a striking, awesome sight. Obviously, it gave a great sense of assurance, confidence, comfort, and security. The people knew beyond any question that God was present with them, there to guide and protect them by day and by night. He was there all the time. Not only was He there, but observe that:

3. The cloud guided the Israelites (v. 17).

"And when the cloud was taken up from the tabernacle, then after that the children of Israel journeyed: and in the place where the cloud abode, there the children of Israel pitched their tents" (Num. 9:17 KJV).

If it lifted and moved, the people followed. If it settled, the people camped. The children of Israel had to move with the cloud. And right now, in this global pandemic when so many are frustrated and confused, the cloud of God's presence is hovering over us, and we need to move with the cloud.

This seems to support the notion that when He says go, we need to go. When He stops, we need to stop. After all, He knows what is best for us, and we need to follow His direction; we need to follow His lead. We need to follow the cloud. Could you declare it aloud: move with the cloud! And the fourth point is a major reason:

4. The cloud was one of the ways the Lord commanded His people—one of the ways He spoke to His people (vv. 18–23).

At His command, that is, as the cloud moved, the people would either set out or stop and camp. Put another way, the children of Israel had their route determined for them. And God wants to determine our route for us. He wants to choose what is best for us. He wants to help us experience His good and perfect will. But we would have to let Him.

Note some thoughts:

1. If the cloud stayed over the Tabernacle, God was commanding His people to remain in the camp (vv. 18–21).

Sometimes they remained in camp for long periods of time, sometimes they stayed for only a few days, and sometimes they remained for only one night. Simply stated, the cloud was one of the ways God used to speak to His people and guide them to the Promised Land.

2. If the cloud lifted by day or by night, they followed (v. 21).

3. If the cloud stayed above the Tabernacle for two days or one month or one year, the people staycd and did not move. But if the cloud lifted, they followed it (v. 22).

4. The people obeyed the Lord's command by the movement of the cloud (v. 23).

They obeyed God's command to camp or travel as He willed. They obeyed God's Word—the movement of the cloud—when instructed by Moses, God's servant. Why? Because the cloud was proof of God's favor that was visible and appreciated by all. We must be careful to obey God's commands and leadership for His guidance to us is proof of His favor. For who He loves, He guides, leads, and gives direction.

Can we take this a little deeper?

5. The fiery cloud was a striking, awesome picture of God's presence and guidance that comes from His Holy Ghost.

(1) Through the power of the Holy Ghost, God is present with His people. He is always present.

Because of the active presence of His Holy Ghost, God never leaves the side of a person who truly believes in Him. God is always with us in an unbroken fellowship, and promises to be with us until we reach the Promised Land of heaven. His presence walks with us day by day.

> For where two or three are gathered together in my name, there am I in the midst of them. (Matt. 18:20)
>
> Lo, I am with you alway, even unto the end of the world. Amen. (Matt. 28:20)

And, behold, I am with thee, and will keep thee in all places whither thou goest, and will bring thee again into this land; for I will not leave thee, until I have done that which I have spoken to thee of. (Gen. 28:15)

[Speaking to Moses, God] "said, My presence shall go with thee, and I will give thee rest. (Exod. 33:14)

When thou goest out to battle against thine enemies, and seest horses, and chariots, and a people more than thou, be not afraid of them: for the Lord thy God is with thee, which brought thee up out of the land of Egypt. (Deut. 20:1)

When thou passest through the waters, I will be with thee; and through the rivers, they shall not overflow thee: when thou walkest through the fire, thou shalt not be burned; neither shall the flame kindle upon thee. (Is. 43:2)

Through the power of the Holy Ghost, God is present with His people. He is always present.

(2) Through the power of The Holy Ghost, God guides His people. He always guides us.

If a person truly believes and follows God, God guides his or her every step day by day. God guides us every step of the way as we march to the Promised Land of heaven.

> Howbeit when he, the Spirit of truth, is come, he will guide you into all truth: for he shall not speak of himself; but whatsoever he shall hear, that shall he speak: and he will show you things to come. (John 16:13)

> He maketh me to lie down in green pastures: he leadeth me beside the still waters. (Ps. 23:2)

> The meek will he guide in judgment: and the meek will he teach his way. (Ps. 25:9)

> For this God is our God for ever and ever: he will be our guide even unto death. (Ps. 48:14)

> Thou shalt guide me with thy counsel, and afterward receive me to glory. (Ps. 73:24)

The prophet Isaiah, speaking of the consistency of God's guidance, said: "And thine ears shall hear a word behind thee, saying, This is the way, walk ye in it, when ye turn to the right hand, and when ye turn to the left" (Isa. 30:21).

Through the power of the Holy Ghost, God guides His people. He always guides us.

Can we go even deeper? You see, The pillar of cloud was representative of the Shekinah glory of God. The cloud of God's presence/ the glory of God's presence hovered, settled, rested, and dwelt above the Tabernacle. The Hebrew words used here to describe Shekinah, actually means the very glory of God dwelling in the midst of His people. Having the Holy Ghost in one's life is proof of the glory of God resting upon that person. Just like the Shekinah glory was the cloud that symbolized God's holy presence, having the Holy Ghost in one's life is proof of having God's presence. This God-sent cloud that had guided Israel out of Egypt was sent to rest upon the Tabernacle as long as His people remained totally obedient to Him.

In the same way, the Shekinah glory of the Holy Ghost and His manifested power has come to rest upon every believer who remains totally obedient to God. The Shekinah glory of God is important in the life of every believer to fight the evil forces of the enemy in these last days. Scripture describes the Shekinah glory of the Lord as follows:

1. **The glory of the Lord is like a consuming fire.**

> "And the sight of the glory of the Lord was like devouring fire on the top of the mount in the eyes of the children of Israel" (Exod. 24:17).

2. The glory of the Lord is like a pillar of fire that radiates light.

"And the Lord went before them by day in a pillar of a cloud, to lead them the way; and by night in a pillar of fire, to give them light; to go by day and night: He took not away the pillar of the cloud by day, nor the pillar of fire by night, from before the people" (Exod. 13:21–22).

3. The glory of the Lord is like a fiery furnace.

"For ye are not come unto the mount that might be touched, and that burned with fire, nor unto blackness, and darkness, and tempest.... For our God is a consuming fire" (Heb. 12:18, 29).

4. The glory of the Lord is like a light that radiates splendor, a light that is so full of splendor that Peter called it "the excellent glory."

"For he received from God the Father honour and glory, when there came such a voice to him from the excellent glory,

This is my beloved Son, in whom I am well pleased" (2 Pet. 1:17).

5. The glory of the Lord is a light so glorious and brilliant that there is no need for a sun.

"Having the glory of God: and her light was like unto a stone most precious, even like a jasper stone, clear as crystal....And the city had no need of the sun, neither of the moon, to shine in it: for the glory of God did lighten it, and the Lamb is the light thereof" (Rev. 21:11, 23).

6. The glory of the Lord is a light so brilliant that no man can approach it.

"Who only hath immortality, dwelling in the light which no man can approach unto; whom no man hath seen, nor can see: to whom be honour and power everlasting" (1 Tim. 6:16).

What am I saying? God wants us to move forward with our spiritual lives, but He wants us doing so under His cloud of leadership and direction. He doesn't want us moving in uncertainty, insecurity, nor doubt. He wants us to move in confidence, fulfilling the purpose for which He has ordained for us to achieve.

God wants us to experience the fire of His Holy Ghost. Experiencing salvation is wonderful. Being baptized with water is great. Being baptized in the Holy Ghost is excellent. But God wants us to experience a new dimension in our relationship with Him. He wants us to step up to a higher level in our spiritual living. He wants us to be baptized in the fire of the Holy Ghost. He wants us to be too hot to handle by the forces unleashed against us by the enemy. He wants us to experience His glory. He wants us to live above spiritual mediocrity. He wants us to fight and win our battles. And this experience of His glory is available to us today. It is simply for the asking. But you must desperately want it. The Prophet Isaiah inspires us: "Arise, shine; for thy light is come, and the glory of the Lord is risen upon thee" (Isa. 60:1 KJV).

This is the season to submit to the glory of the Lord that has risen upon you. This is the ideal time to give yourself to the power of the Spirit. This is the time to let the glory of the

Chapter Seven

Spirit of God rest upon you and give you direction in your life. He wants to guide you. He wants to lead you. You must open up your spirit to receive Him. He is here, and He is waiting for you to let Him take full control of your life. Would you bow your head now and receive Him? Would you pause now and submit to Him? He is the greatest gift you can ever have in this world.

Chapter Eight

Move Forward by Putting God First

The Lord our God said to us at Horeb, "You have stayed long enough at this mountain. Break camp and advance into the hill country of the Amorites; go to all the neighboring peoples in the Arabah. (Deut. 1:6–7a NIV)

The Lord our God spake unto us in Horeb, saying, Ye have dwelt long enough in this mount. (Deu. 1:6 KJV)

Speak unto the children of Israel, and say unto them, When ye be come into the land which I give unto you, and shall reap the harvest thereof, then ye shall bring a sheaf of the firstfruits of your harvest unto the priest. (Lev. 23:10 KJV)

Confession: (Passionately affirm): *I move forward by putting God first in my life! He is the first of the harvest, and the first to arise from the dead!*

Introduction

Each year, many of our congregations gather fruits and vegetables from persons in our community to bring them into the house of God. We arrange these items to make beautiful displays and decorations in such lovely ways.

We recite well written poems and sing wonderful songs as we celebrate Harvest Thanksgiving in the form of a program. But Harvest thanksgiving services are more than traditional ceremonies. For believers, they should represent greater spiritual significance and meaning.

The above referenced passage speaks of the Festival of Firstfruits (Lev. 23:9–14). This was a festival to thank God for the crops, for the harvest of food that had given life to the people. This celebration was a festival that commentated

Christ Himself. It was a celebration that was symbolic of the work that Christ did for all believers. For two major reasons. First, He is the first of the harvest, the first to arise from the dead; and second, He is the one who had given real life to the people. (More about this later.)

But note that this festival could not begin until the people had entered the *Promised Land* (v. 10).

There are certain blessings God's people cannot obtain unless they are positioned in the place where they ought to be. The people had to enter the Promised Land. The people had to have been at a place of special rest, a place of spiritual advancement, a place of having attained some spiritual advancement in their journey. They had to enter the Promised Land of God to be able to participate. God said to Moses: "Speak unto the children of Israel, and say unto them, *When ye be come into the land which I give unto you*, and shall reap the harvest thereof, then ye shall bring a sheaf of the firstfruits of your harvest unto the priest." (Lev. 23:10)

They, of course, could not plant crops out in the desert while they were marching to the Promised Land. But once they arrived and began planting crops, they were to give the first of their harvest to the Lord during this festival.

Note further that *the people were also required to first produce fruit*.

Verse 10 states: "Speak unto the children of Israel, and say unto them, When ye be come into the land which I give unto you, *and shall reap the harvest thereof*, then ye shall bring a sheaf of the firstfruits of your harvest unto the priest."

This suggests that the people had to have been productive already. This means that they would have had to progress in their spiritual journey enough to produce fruit. Put another way, there had to have been a certain level of spiritual maturity and production in order for them to give back to God and His servant (the priest). And when they gave, they were to take a sheaf, that is, a bundle of grain stalks, here and there, bundle it together, tie it, and bring it to the priest. He was then to take the sheaf and wave it as an offering before the Lord. This was to be done on the day after the Sabbath, which would be Sunday. And after giving the wave offering to the Lord, the priest was to approach God for atonement through a special burnt offering.

It is also important to note that a special grain offering was to be offered to the Lord two times larger than usual. Consider the result: the aroma of the burning sacrifice and grain offering ascended up, symbolizing God's acceptance. He would be pleased with the aroma of the sacrifice, the obedience of the people. However, there was one clear prohibition, one clear rule, one clear law: *the people had to put God first.* They were not to eat any of the harvest until the firstfruit offering was given to God. This was to be a permanent law for all the generations to come, no matter where the Israelites lived.

Can I just pause a little to emphasize two things?

1. **The believer is to give God the first of his or her harvest.**

This includes the first of the believer's income. Every believer is to give his or her tithe, for the tithe belongs to the Lord. The tithe should be an expression of appreciation and thanksgiving to God, for God is the one who has given us all that we have. Our crops and jobs are due to Him; so is our health that enables us to work and earn a living. We are to give the firstfruit to support the church and the messengers of the gospel around the world so that they can reach the world for Christ. Having a Harvest Thanksgiving service is to remind us of this. God's Word still resonates loud and clear: we are to "seek first His Kingdom and His righteousness and all other things will be added unto us." (Matt. 6:33)

We are called to put God first!

> Upon the first day of the week let every one of you lay by him in store, as God hath prospered him, that there be no gatherings when I come. (1 Cor. 16:2)

But this I say, He which soweth sparingly shall reap also sparingly; and he which soweth bountifully shall reap also bountifully. Every man according as he purposeth in his heart, so let him give; not grudgingly, or of necessity: for God loveth a cheerful giver. (2 Cor. 9:6–7)

And all the tithe of the land, whether of the seed of the land, or of the fruit of the tree, is the Lord's: it is holy unto the Lord. (Lev. 27:30)

Every man shall give as he is able, according to the blessing of the Lord thy God which he hath given thee. (Dec. 16:17)

Bring ye all the tithes into the storehouse, that there may be meat in mine house, and prove me now herewith, saith the Lord of hosts, if I will not open you the windows of heaven, and pour you out a blessing, that there shall not be room enough to receive it. (Mal. 3:10)

The believer is to give God the first of his harvest, the first of his income. But note a second point.

2. The Festival of Firstfruits is also a symbol of the Lord's resurrection.

Christ is the first of the harvest, the first to arise from the dead. It is Jesus Christ and His resurrection that give the believer hope of arising from the dead to live eternally with God. The prophetic picture of salvation is this:

(1) The Passover (that was first practiced in Egypt, protecting God's people from death) symbolized the believer's deliverance or redemption from the world.

(2) The Festival of Unleavened Bread symbolized the urgency of the believer to leave the world to begin his march to the Promised Land.

(3) The Festival of Firstfruits symbolizes the glorious hope the believer has as he marches toward the Promised Land, the hope of being raised from the dead to live eternally with God—all because of the resurrection of Christ.

> That Christ should suffer, and that he should be the first that should rise from the dead, and should show light unto the people, and to the Gentiles. (Acts 26:23)

> But now is Christ risen from the dead, and become the firstfruits of them that slept. For since by man came death, by man came also the resurrection of the

dead. For as in Adam all die, even so in Christ shall all be made alive. But every man in his own order: Christ the firstfruits; afterward they that are Christ's at his coming. (1 Cor. 15:20–23)

Knowing that he which raised up the Lord Jesus shall raise up us also by Jesus, and shall present us with you. (2 Cor. 4:14)

The apostle Peter agreed when he said:

Blessed be the God and Father of our Lord Jesus Christ, which according to his abundant mercy hath begotten us again unto a lively hope by the resurrection of Jesus Christ from the dead, To an inheritance incorruptible, and undefiled, and that fadeth not away, reserved in heaven for you. (1 Pet. 1:3–4)

What is the point? When we gather fruits and vegetables and celebrate Harvest Thanksgiving, we are commemorating the Festival of Firstfruits. We are celebrating Jesus Christ, the first of the harvest who was first risen from the dead. And because of this, we too have hope of a blessed resurrection from death into eternal life. For this, Our God deserves praise!

Chapter Nine

Move Forward: Acknowledge God as Your Refuge and Strength

God is our refuge and strength, a very present help in trouble.

Therefore, will not we fear, though the earth be removed, and though the mountains be carried into the midst of the sea;

Though the waters thereof roar and be troubled, though the mountains shake with the swelling thereof. Selah. (Ps. 46:1–3 KJV)

Confession (Affirm with boldness): *I declare that Jehovah God is my refuge and strength!*

Introduction

Most of us are familiar with the story of Job, for we often associate him with trouble. After Job was battered by a series of devastating tragedies, his friends traveled a great distance to be with him. And the Bible tells us that they sat silently with him for seven days and seven nights, staying by his side during his immeasurable grief. Job finally broke the silence, saying, "The thing which I greatly feared is come upon me" (Job 3:25). With this statement, Job lamented that the worst tragedy he could imagine had come to pass.

Many of us have wondered what we would do if a terrible tragedy occurred in our lives. For some, this would be the death of a spouse or, perhaps even worse, the loss of a child. For others, it would be a diagnosis of cancer or the loss of mental capacity. Yet for others, it would be a fire or some other catastrophic natural disaster. And now, globally it is the eminent threat of infection of the coronavirus (COVID-19).

Psalm 46 was written during a time of overwhelming turmoil in Jerusalem. Many scholars believe the setting for this psalm, along with Psalms 47 and 48, is the Assyrian invasion of Judah during Hezekiah's reign. Some even think that Hezekiah himself wrote these psalms. But whatever the case, we know that it was a time of fierce trouble and that God protected and gloriously delivered His people from it.

Psalm 46 was such an important song that it was committed to the care of the chief musician, with the instruction *alamoth*. This likely means it was to be performed by high-pitched voices or, more specifically, by young women. However, it could also mean it was to be accompanied by high-pitched stringed instruments (1 Chron. 15:20). We all make daily plans to help us enjoy our lives; and we live in hope, expecting them to succeed. The reality is, however, at some point in our lives, we will face circumstances we feel are more than we can handle; overwhelming situations which seem too much for us to bare. Some time or the other, we will know the hollow, helpless feeling of being able to do nothing to change our situation. And having the threat of COVID-19 and the other variants seem to be such a time.

Notice how this threat has affected us. In a matter of weeks, the entire world as we knew it was changed. And millions, the world over, are still losing heart in fear. But I believe that the Lord has given us Psalm 46 for times like these. This great psalm was said to be the inspiration for Martin Luther's great hymn, "A Mighty Fortress Is Our God"—a bulwark never failing! And thank God, He still is a Mighty Fortress, able to stem the tide of every evil attack on the lives of His children! We praise Him for that!

This is a psalm that points us to the superior power of God when facing devastating misfortune or overwhelming trouble. The psalm seems to lend itself to at least four divisions of encouragement as follows:

First, the writer encourages us to:

1. Confess God as your refuge and strength (vv. 1–3).
2. Rest assured of God's presence and power (vv. 4–7).
3. Behold the works of the Lord: a picture of the last days (vv. 8–9).

4. Be still—wait and hope in the Lord—the Lord is God (vv. 10–11).

But we will focus on the first segment of the psalm and the first three verses only.

First, you are encouraged to …

1. Confess God as your refuge and strength (Ps. 46:1–3).

As a terrifying crisis approached Jerusalem, the psalmist led God's people to lean fully on the Lord. With the calmness that only faith can give, he confessed that God was their refuge and strength. A refuge is a shelter, that is, a place where we can hide for protection. Strength as used here, speaks of the power that God gives us to endure and overcome adversity. And so, when faced with difficulties and disorder in our lives, God wants His children to confess who He is. He is our refuge! He is our strength! He is our present help in times of trouble!

Let the enemy know who He is. After all, He is power, and He is might. He is our Master, our Lord, our Savior, our Redeemer, our Friend, our Deliverer, our Healer, our Protector, our Provider, our Buckler, our Shield, our Defender, and our Sustainer. He is still the answer to all the problems that life presents. And so, whatever challenge we face in our daily lives, He wants us to confess who He is. Our confession is important for it affirms our faith in a mighty, able God, and what we say is what we get.

And so, note two reasons why He wants you to confess Him as your refuge and strength.

He wants us to confess Him as our refuge and strength because:

a. He is always ready to help us in times of trouble (v. 1).

Note the verse: "*God is our refuge and strength, a very present help in trouble.*"

The Hebrew word for trouble literally means a narrow or tight place where a person is unable to move, a tight spot (if you please). It is also used to describe severe pressure. We have all been exposed to tight spots and severe pressure in our lives. We all face situations beyond our control, but we do not have to face them alone. When trouble strikes, God is present.

He is present, even in the most difficult storms of our lives. In fact, He is always there with us, immediately available to help us when trouble arises. He is not just a present help in times of trouble but a *very* present help in times of trouble. The adverb *very* indicates that He is exceedingly or speedily present to assist us. He comes to us quickly. He comes to us efficiently. He deals with our situation effectively. Not even a second goes by when we have to face our troubles alone or in our own strength. In the words of an anonymous writer, published since 1892:

"No! Never alone! No! Never alone! He promised never to leave me, never to leave me alone!"

God is with you, and He is ready to help you (in your time of trouble).

b. He will enable us to conquer fear, even in the most catastrophic circumstances (vv. 2–3).

These verses read: *"Therefore will not we fear, though the earth be removed, and though the mountains be carried into the midst of the sea;*

Though the waters thereof roar and be troubled, though the mountains shake with the swelling thereof. Selah."

The psalmist took great care to assure us that we need not fear when trouble strikes. Disasters that shake the earth to its core cannot shake us when we take refuge in the Lord. Referring to four types of natural disasters, the psalmist described some of the fiercest catastrophes imaginable:

- Earthquakes so powerful they alter the face of the earth and cause the ground to completely collapse beneath us (v. 2a)
- Hurricanes so strong and long-lasting that even the mountains are immersed in water (v. 2b)
- Massive tidal waves or tsunamis repeatedly crashing against the land (v. 3a)
- Fiery volcanic eruptions from mountains surging or swelling with lava (v. 3b).

Regardless of the accident or natural catastrophe, God's Word assures that He will be with us, so we need not fear. These natural calamities also point to the day of the Lord when God's judgment will fall upon the earth, leading up to the return and reign of Christ. Yet, the Psalmist encourages that in these times of violent disasters, we must declare who our God is for He will deliver us and conquer our fears.

We should live day by day with the understanding that life in this sin-cursed world is full of trouble (Job 5:7; 14:1: Eccles. 2:23). And trouble assumes many forms:

- sickness or injury
- the death of a loved one
- marriage problems
- rebellion or disobedience by our children
- war.

And when serious problems occur in our lives, our first tendency can be to panic or fear. We might immediately become anxious, fretting over what may happen or what we are going to do. When we realize there is nothing we can do, our panic and fear might even increase. But instead of fearing and fretting, let us remember that we do not face the situation alone but with

God's presence and help. Through every experience, God is with us. As believers, God's Spirit lives within us. Therefore, He is always with us.

When trouble attacks, we do not have to wait for God to arrive; He is already there. Instead of attempting to deal with difficulties in our own strength, we need to flee to God for shelter and strength. We should not speak out of doubt or unbelief, but with full faith in God's love and care for us. We must trust Him boldly with full understanding that He is a dependable God. He stands ready to help us through any and all of our trials.

Of all the human emotions, fear may be the most crippling. But fear can be overcome when we understand that the one who is greater than all our troubles is with us. And He has given us His Spirit to combat the spirit of fear (2 Tim. 1:7). He will protect us; He will strengthen us and use the challenges of life to mold us into the image of His Son.

The apostle Paul to his spiritual son, Timothy encouraged him:

"For God hath not given us the spirit of fear; but of power, and of love, and of a sound mind" (2 Tim. 1:7)

God assured Joshua: "Have not I commanded thee? Be strong and of a good courage; be not afraid, neither be thou dismayed: for the Lord thy God is with thee whithersoever thou goest" (Josh. 1:9).

Through His prophet Isaiah God admonishes: "Fear thou not; for I am with thee: be not dismayed; for I am thy God: I will strengthen thee; yea, I will help thee; yea, I will uphold thee with the right hand of my righteousness" (Isa. 41:10 KJV).

In Isaiah 43:2, He promises: "When thou passest through the waters, I will be with thee; and through the rivers, they shall not overflow thee: when thou walkest through the fire, thou shalt not be burned; neither shall the flame kindle upon thee."

Psalm 93:4 reminds us that "The LORD on high is mightier than the noise of many waters, yea, than the mighty waves of the sea" (Ps. 93:4).

And in Psalm 145 we are encouraged to call out to God! "The LORD is nigh unto all them that call upon him, to all that call upon him in truth" (Ps. 145:18).

Concluding thoughts

Our world is in turmoil. But in this time of overwhelming trouble, the Psalmist confidently affirmed: "I will say of the LORD, He is my refuge and my fortress: my God; in him will I trust" (Ps. 91:2). And so, in this time of global panic and upheaval over COVID-19 and its variants, what do you say? As I close, I want to challenge you a little. First, you must acknowledge that the time is here when true faith in God must be activated.

The time has come for our long-standing profession (those things we have claimed to believe for years as Christians) to be tested. Do you really believe those things you have professed for years? Well, do you? These end-time events of increased birth pains and the beginning of sorrows (as described in Matthew 24) must spur us into a greater dimension of preparations and anointing for the church to begin to operate as the Church. No longer can any of us hide behind our frequent visits to a building of worship to validate who we are for opportunities to do so can be curtailed. Instead, we must now, in the privacy of our homes, be the true Church (part of that holy body of believers, saved by the precious blood of the Lamb) and conduct our private worship in sincerity. No longer can any of us depend on any minister to lay hands on us to pray for us or otherwise administer to us. But we must now, in the privacy of our homes, lay hands on ourselves, minister to ourselves, and pray for ourselves. No longer can any of us try to impress each other by our pious appearance and mannerisms when we gather together. But we must now, in the privacy of our homes, be our true selves in the presence of the all-seeing, Holy God. The time has come for us to realize that we are the church!

This is a time of serious spiritual evaluation. In this time when we are faced with global wars, this pandemic and economic uncertainty, it is an ideal time to ask ourselves: "Having claimed to be a Christian for years, Can I truly *confess God as my refuge and strength? Do I really have such a relationship with Him?*"

If your answer is no, He can help you. You can establish a relationship with God through

His Son Jesus and begin anew. In this critical climate, He wants you to entrust your life to Him. He is ready to help you in this time of trouble. Would you let Him?

Let us pray:

Father God, in this time of global upheaval and confusion, we are grateful that we can find refuge in You. We acknowledge that we have drifted away from your holy standards in our living, and we ask your forgiveness. We ask that Your Son, Jesus, would come and take His aboard in our lives, providing us with the comfort and direction we so desperately need in this hour. We surrender our lives to You and trust You to move us forward serving with excellence. Thank You for hearing and answering us, in Jesus's name. Amen!

About the Author

Dr. Samuel U. Daniel is a Christian counselling psychologist and life coach. He is the founding director of Daniel's Counselling Services at the Hughes Medical Center, Anguilla, and the founding president of "It Takes Two Ministries. He serves as Overseer of three congregations, is a fellow of Cambridge University, England, as well as an adjunct lecturer at the Anguilla Community

College. He has earned degrees and certificates from several institutions including College of Further Education, St. Kitts; University of the West Indies, Jamaica; The United Theological College of the West Indies, Jamaica; Cambridge University, England, UK; Friends Christian University, California; and Atlantic Coast Graduate School of Theology, Florida. He is married to Malita for thirty-eight years and together they have two young adult children, Jervayne and Samalta.

CPSIA information can be obtained
at www.ICGtesting.com
Printed in the USA
BVHW020348110622
639545BV00016B/456